Animals in the Fall

by
Gail Saunders-Smith

Pebble Books
an imprint of Capstone Press

Pebble Books

Pebble Books are published by Capstone Press
818 North Willow Street, Mankato, Minnesota 56001
http://www.capstone-press.com
Copyright © 1998 by Capstone Press

Library of Congress Cataloging-in-Publication Data
Saunders-Smith, Gail.
  Animals in the fall/by Gail Saunders-Smith.
    p. cm.
  Includes bibliographical references (p. 23) and index.
  Summary: Simple text and photographs present the behavior
changes of animals as winter approaches, such as growing
thicker fur, migrating, and hibernating.
  ISBN 1-56065-588-7
  1. Animal behavior--Juvenile literature. 2. Animal
migration--Juvenile literature. 3. Autumn--Juvenile literature.
[1. Animals--Habits and behavior. 2. Animals--Migration.
3. Autumn.] I. Title.

QL751.5.S38 1998
591.56--dc21   97-29804
                                   CIP
                                   AC

Editorial Credits
Lois Wallentine, editor; Timothy Halldin and James Franklin,
design; Michelle L. Norstad, photo research

Photo Credits
Bonefish Nature Images/Mark Morin, 10, 12
Michael H. Francis, 1, 14, 16, 18
Cathy and Gordon Illg, 4
Innerspace Visions/Doug Perrine, 8
Lior Rubin, 6
Unicorn Stock/Pam Power, cover; John Ebling, 20

Table of Contents

Geese fly south.

Some butterflies
fly south.

Some whales
swim south.

10

Deer grow winter coats.

Some dogs grow
winter coats.

Some rabbits grow
winter coats.

Squirrels build nests.

Beavers build
lodges.

19

Bears find dens.

Words to Know

bear—a large, heavy animal with thick fur

beaver—an animal with a wide, flat tail that builds dams across streams to create its lodge

butterfly—a thin insect with large, often brightly colored wings

deer—an animal with hooves

goose—a large bird with a long neck and webbed feet

rabbit—a small animal with long ears

squirrel—a small animal with a bushy tail

whale—a large sea animal that looks like a fish

Read More

Fowler, Allan. *How Do You Know It's Fall?* Chicago: Children's Press, 1992.

Fowler, Allan. *Squirrels and Chipmunks.* Chicago: Children's Press, 1997.

My First Look at Seasons. New York: Random House, 1990.

Internet Sites

Journey North 1997
http://www.learner.org/content/k12/jnorth

Searching Animal Diversity Web
http://www.oit.itd.umich.edu/bio/
   biogate-p.cgi/bio/bio.index

Note to Parents and Teachers

This book illustrates and describes the changes and behavior of animals as winter approaches. The clear photographs support the beginning reader in making and maintaining the meaning of the text. All noun and verb changes are clearly depicted in the photographs. Children may need assistance in using the Table of Contents, Words to Know, Read More, Internet Sites, and Index/Word List sections of the book.

Index/Word List

Word Count: 34